JUL   2009

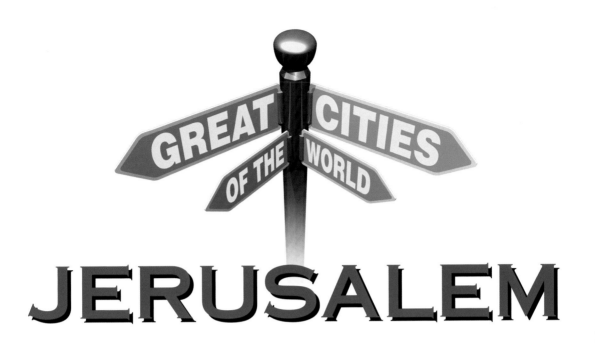

JERUSALEM

ROB BOWDEN

WORLD ALMANAC® LIBRARY

Please visit our web site at: www.worldalmanaclibrary.com
For a free color catalog describing World Almanac® Library's list of high-quality books
and multimedia programs, call 1-800-848-2928 (USA) or 1-800-387-3178 (Canada).
World Almanac® Library's fax: (414) 332-3567.

Library of Congress Cataloging-in-Publication Data

Bowden, Rob.
    Jerusalem / by Rob Bowden.
       p. cm. — (Great cities of the world)
    Includes bibliographical references and index.
    ISBN 0-8368-5051-3 (lib.bdg.)
    ISBN 0-8368-5211-7 (softcover)
    1. Jerusalem—History—Juvenile literature. 2. Jerusalem—Social life and customs—
Juvenile literature. 3. Jerusalem—Ethnic relations—Juvenile literature. I. Title. II. Series.
    DS109.9.B65   2005
    956.94'42—dc22   2005043586

First published in 2006 by
World Almanac® Library
A Member of the WRC Media Family of Companies
330 West Olive Street, Suite 100
Milwaukee, WI 53212 USA

Produced by Discovery Books
Editors: Betsy Rasmussen and Kathryn Walker
Series designers: Laurie Shock, Keith Williams
Designer and page production: Rob Norridge
Photo researcher: Rachel Tisdale
Diagrams: Rob Norridge
Maps: Stefan Chabluk
World Almanac® Library editorial direction: Mark J. Sachner
World Almanac® Library editor: Gini Holland
World Almanac® Library art direction: Tammy West
World Almanac® Library graphic design: Scott M. Krall
World Almanac® Library production: Jessica Morris

Cover: In Jerusalem's old city, the golden dome of Islam's third-holiest site, the Dome of the Rock, rises above the
massive Western Wall, or "Wailing Wall," of the Temple Mount, Judaism's holiest site.

Printed in Canada

1 2 3 4 5 6 7 8 9 09 08 07 06 05

Contents

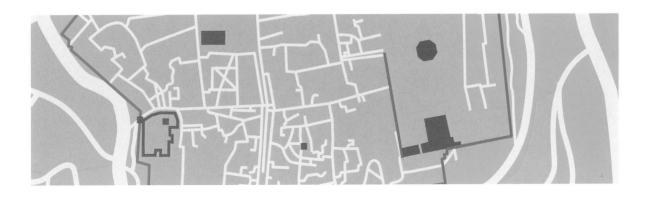

Introduction

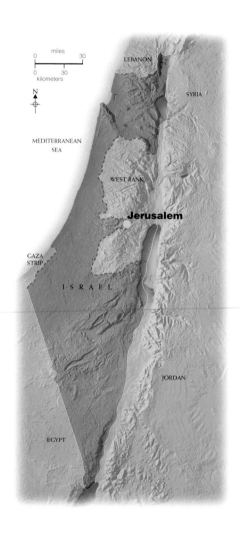

Frequently referred to as the world's holiest city, Jerusalem is a spiritual center for three of the world's major

◄ The distinctive cityscape of Jerusalem, with the Dome of the Rock at its center, is seen here from the Mount of Olives.

◄ The red dotted line on this map shows the boundaries of Israel that are recognized by most countries in the international community. East Jerusalem, the West Bank, and the Gaza Strip have been occupied by Israel since 1967 but are not internationally recognized as parts of Israel.

religions: Judaism, Christianity, and Islam. All three religions lay claim to Jerusalem, and this has been a source of debate and conflict for thousands of years. In more recent decades, the claims to Jerusalem have polarized into a tense and often violent contest between the mainly Jewish state of Israel and the Palestinian people, who are predominantly Muslim.

"Ten measures of beauty were bestowed upon the world; nine were taken by Jerusalem and one by the rest of the world."

—Babylonian Talmud, sixth century.

Contested City

At one time in recent history, East Jerusalem belonged to the country of Jordan and was inhabited largely by Palestinians. In 1967, Israel fought a war against Jordan and other Arab states and gained control of East Jerusalem. Israel considers Jerusalem reunited and continues to claim the entire city as its rightful capital. The Palestinians, however, believe that the Israelis are

CITY FACTS

Jerusalem
Capital of Israel (recognized as such by U.S. and other nations; disputed by Palestinians and others)

Founded: 1000 B.C.

Area (Metropolitan): 49 square miles (126 square kilometers)

Population (Metropolitan): 680,400 (census 2002)

Population Density: 13,886 people per square mile (5,400 people per sq km)

illegally occupying their land and that East Jerusalem should become the capital of a newly declared Palestinian state. So important is Jerusalem as a symbol to both groups that neither has been willing to back down. Therefore, at the start of the twenty-first century, the competing claims to Jerusalem remain unresolved, and the city may well be the world's most contested piece of land.

Geography

Jerusalem, located in the Judean Hills of Israel and the West Bank, sits at an altitude of 2,654 feet (809 meters). Unlike most cities, Jerusalem does not possess natural geographical qualities that make it a desirable location for a settlement, such as

Municipality of Jerusalem

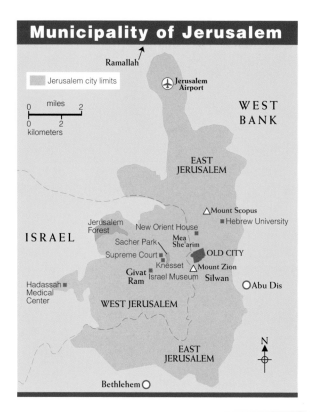

▲ Along with other land formerly belonging to Jordan (including the present-day West Bank), East Jerusalem was annexed by Israel in 1967. Many nations do not recognize it as Israeli territory. The red dotted line in this map indicates the internationally recognized boundaries of Jerusalem. The city limits, shown in purple, were designated by Israel. The area within the city limits is the Municipality of Jerusalem.

Climate

Because of its altitude in the Judean Hills, Jerusalem avoids the scorching heat that sizzles throughout much of the rest of the Middle East. Four distinct seasons unfold in Jerusalem. Winter (mid-November through mid-March) is the wettest time of year in Jerusalem, accounting for about 85 percent of the average annual precipitation—January and February alone receive about 10.4 inches (264 millimeters) of precipitation, or 50 percent of the total. Winter months are also the coolest months, with temperatures dropping as low as 27° Fahrenheit (-3° Celsius), but averaging about 48° F (9° C). Spring (mid-March through May) sees the last of the winter rains and a sharp increase in temperatures to about 70° F (21° C) on average. A warm wind called the khamsin can blow from the Sahara Desert during spring and increase temperatures to near 104° F (40° C). Summer (June through September) is hot and dry with daily temperatures averaging about 86° F (30° C). Autumn (October through November) sees the start of winter rains, occasional khamsin winds, and temperatures similar to spring.

fertile plains, a good water supply, or river or ocean access. It is the religious significance of Jerusalem, from its earliest days, that has drawn people to the city and led to its growth.

Three main areas can be identified in Jerusalem: the old city, East Jerusalem, and West Jerusalem. The old city lies to the east

of today's city center and is clearly marked by city walls that surround it. Within its walls, the old city is divided into four quarters—Jewish, Muslim, Christian, and Armenian (Orthodox Christians)—each with its own distinctive character. A labyrinth of narrow alleyways connects the

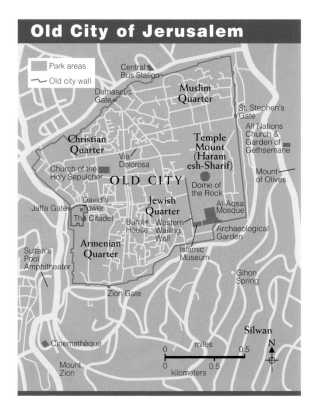

Old City of Jerusalem

Park areas
Old city wall

Central Bus Station
Damascus Gate
Muslim Quarter
St. Stephen's Gate
All Nations Church & Garden of Gethsemane
Christian Quarter
Via Dolorosa
Temple Mount (Haram esh-Sharif)
Church of the Holy Sepulcher
OLD CITY
Dome of the Rock
Mount of Olives
David's Tower
Jaffa Gate
The Citadel
Jewish Quarter
Al-Aqsa Mosque
Burnt House
Western Wailing Wall
Archaeological Garden
Sultan's Pool Amphitheater
Armenian Quarter
Islamic Museum
Zion Gate
Gihon Spring
Silwan
Cinemathèque
miles 0   0.5
N
Mount Zion
kilometers 0   0.5

four quarters and the city's many religious sites. These include the Western Wailing Wall (Judaism's most holy site), the Dome of the Rock (Islam's third-holiest site), and the Church of the Holy Sepulcher (Christianity's most sacred site).

West Jerusalem, or the new city, extends to the west and is the commercial and governmental center of the city. East Jerusalem is an older part of the city and is where the majority of Jerusalem's Arab population lives and works.

▶ *The Church of the Holy Sepulcher, pictured here, is the most sacred site in Christendom and has attracted Christian pilgrims for more than one thousand years.*

CHAPTER 1

History of Jerusalem

Interpretations of Jerusalem's history lie at the heart of contested claims to the city and are a source of continuing debate among historians. One thing that can be agreed upon, however, is that Jerusalem's history is long and complicated and has often been characterized by violence.

Ancient Origins

The oldest evidence of a human settlement in Jerusalem dates back to between 3000 and 2500 B.C. Archaeologists discovered walls of an old city close to Gihon Spring. The spring would have provided early settlers with a water supply in this otherwise desert environment. These early settlers are thought to have been nomadic Amorites (or Canaanites) who arrived here from Arabia to the east. The Amorites worshiped a god they called Shalem, and this is thought to be the origin of the name Jerusalem, which means "city or foundation of Shalem." Ancient Egyptian texts dating from the twentieth to the fourteenth centuries B.C. also note the existence of Jerusalem as a city-state controlled by the Jebusites (closely related to Amorites).

◀ *The lights of the early evening illuminate the old walled city of Jerusalem with the modern city visible beyond.*

City of David

In 1000 B.C., King David united the twelve tribes of northern Israel and southern Judah for the first time and claimed Jerusalem as the capital of his new kingdom. Jerusalem provided a neutral location between the lands of these twelve tribes. It was fortified on three sides by the Judean Hills to protect it from attack, and the Gihon Spring provided its people with a source of freshwater. Some religions believe that during his reign, King David brought to Jerusalem the Ark of the Covenant—the shrine containing the tablets of law said to have been given to Moses on Mount Sinai.

As David sought a location for a temple to house the ark, some believe that God revealed Mount Moriah to him. It was on Mount Moriah about one thousand years earlier that God was said to have spoken to Abraham, the patriarch of the Jewish people, and prevented him from sacrificing his son. As Ibrahim, Abraham is also a patriarch of Islam. These associations with the area laid the foundation for Jerusalem as one of the holiest places in the world. Upon David's

> *"It's almost impossible to write a book on Jerusalem without offending someone. It's literally like writing in a minefield; you never know when your pen will set off a mine."*
>
> —Eric Cline, *Jerusalem Besieged: From Ancient Canaan to Modern Israel*, 2004.

▲ *This mosaic, dating from about A.D. 432 to 444, depicts the Israelites transporting the Ark of the Covenant to the city of Jerusalem.*

death, his son Solomon took the throne and oversaw the building of the First Temple on Mount Moriah, completed in 953 B.C. Today, this location is called Temple Mount.

Years of Turmoil

Following the death of King Solomon in 922 B.C., the kingdom of David split, with ten northern tribes leaving Jerusalem and forming the Kingdom of Israel. The two remaining tribes formed the Kingdom of Judah and retained Jerusalem as their capital. The Judeans (Jews) did not retain control of Jerusalem for long, however, and the city periodically fell under Egyptian, Philistine, and Arabian control in the period leading up to 687 B.C. Jerusalem was then conquered by the Assyrians and later the Babylonians, whose King Nebuchadnezzer destroyed the First Temple in 586 B.C. and exiled the Jews. The Persians conquered the Babylonians in 538 B.C. and allowed the Jews to return to Jerusalem and rebuild their temple, which was completed in 515 B.C.

In about 333 B.C., the armies of Alexander the Great arrived in Jerusalem, and its people peacefully surrendered to become part of the Greek empire under the Ptolemies of Egypt. In 198 B.C., the Seleucids (a rival Greek power based in Syria) ousted the Ptolemies and set about transforming Jerusalem into a Hellenistic (Greek) city. Two of the actions included in this transformation were rededicating the temple to the Greek god Zeus and sacrificing pigs across its altar. These actions insulted the Jews of Jerusalem, and, in 167 B.C., a Jewish revolt began, led by five brothers from the House of Hasmon. In 164 B.C., Jews regained control of the temple and reinstated their control of Jerusalem under the Hasmonean dynasty.

The Romans and Christ

Ideological rifts within the Jewish community left Jerusalem in a weakened state, and the Roman armies of Pompey captured the city in 63 B.C. to begin a period of Roman rule that lasted until the seventh century A.D. In 40 B.C., Herod became ruler there, and Jerusalem reached its ancient

▲ Herod the Great, pictured here in an engraving, oversaw a period of great prosperity in ancient Palestine and made Jerusalem into one of the finest cities in the world.

historical population peak with about one hundred thousand people. Herod is well known for expanding the city's temple to make it one of the finest of the ancient world. The work, undertaken by ten thousand workers, included expanding the temple grounds with enormous reinforcing walls. One of these walls is the Western Wall that is today the holiest site of Judaism. Shortly after Herod's death in 4 B.C., Rome chose to rule Jerusalem more directly through procurators (administrative officials). It was one of these procurators, Pontius Pilate, who was responsible for the crucifixion of Jesus.

Jesus was one of many orators who frequented Jerusalem and voiced criticism against, among other things, Roman control of the city, market activities in the temple, and the exploitation of the poor by wealthy Jerusalemites loyal to the Romans. Jesus was arrested for crimes against the state. Found guilty, Jesus was sentenced by Pontius Pilate to death by crucifixion in the year A.D. 33.

In A.D. 66, a Jewish uprising began that led to a war between Jews and Romans and resulted in the Romans destroying Jerusalem together with its Second Temple in A.D. 70.

▼ *The Western Wall in Jerusalem is all that remains of the Second Temple and is the most sacred site for Jews. It is also known as the "Wailing Wall" because of the sorrow Jewish people have felt for the loss of their temple.*

Jews continued to worship on the ruins of the temple, and that prompted the Emperor Hadrian to completely destroy Jerusalem and build a new city, Aelia Capitolina, upon its ruins in A.D. 135. The street layout of what is now considered Jerusalem's old city dates to this time, as does the placement of the city walls. Hadrian banned Jews from entering the city, and this led to a division in which, by some accounts, the followers of Jesus chose to distance themselves from Judaism in order to gain access to the city. They changed the Sabbath from Saturday to Sunday, for example. This group, who believed Jesus to be the Messiah, were the first Christians.

A Christian City

Jerusalem's rise as a Christian city came when Constantine the Great (288–337) adopted Christianity as the official faith of the Byzantine Roman Empire. His mother, Empress Helena, made a pilgrimage to Jerusalem in 326 in order to search for the holy sites related to the life of Jesus. She identified what she believed to be the place of his crucifixion, and Constantine ordered the construction of the Church of the Holy Sepulcher upon this site (the present Church of the Holy Sepulcher was built in phases from 1042 because the original was destroyed in 1009). For about three hundred years, Jerusalem grew and prospered as a Christian city. Many fine churches, monasteries, and hospices were built, and Jerusalem became a major destination for Christian pilgrims.

A Muslim City

In 638, the armies of the Caliph ("successor to Mohammed") Omar, assisted by local Jews, besieged Jerusalem, ousted the Christian Byzantines, and introduced Islam to the city. Jerusalem became especially important to Islam as it was said to be the

▼ *The Dome of the Rock on Temple Mount (Haram esh-Sharif) was built in the seventh century and is the oldest building in Islam.*

"It may be called the City of Peace, but no other city has been more bitterly fought over than Jerusalem. In the past 4,000 years it has seen at least 118 conflicts. It has been razed at least twice, has been besieged 23 times, and has had at least five separate periods of violent terrorist attacks in the past century."

—Eric Cline, *Jerusalem Besieged: From Ancient Canaan to Modern Israel*, 2004.

▲ *This picture of Jerusalem was painted in the fifteenth century, a period when it was a predominantly Islamic city.*

place from where the prophet Mohammed embarked on his night journey to pray with God. The exact location of Mohammed's departure was said to be from the rock on Temple Mount, and so Caliph Omar declared the Temple Mount as a place of Muslim worship. Haram esh-Sharif, as Muslims knew it, became the third-holiest place of Islam (after Mecca and Medina) and has retained that status to this day. Between 685 and 691, Caliph Abd al-Malik built the Dome of the Rock to house the rock from where Mohammed made his ascent. The Dome of the Rock is one of the oldest surviving Muslim buildings in the world. Al Aqsa Mosque and other Islamic architecture in Jerusalem can also be dated to this period.

For more than three hundred years, the Islamic rulers of Jerusalem tolerated Christians and Jews, but by the end of the tenth century this tolerance had been replaced with persecution and the destruction of Christian and Jewish holy sites. In 1071, the Seljuk Turks conquered the holy lands and blockaded Christian

13

"The air above Jerusalem is filled with
*   prayers and dreams*
Like the air above cities with heavy
*   industry*
Hard to breathe"

—Yehuda Amichai, "Jerusalem Ecology," 1980.

pilgrims from visiting Jerusalem and its holy sites. The blockade sparked a series of Christian crusades in which Jerusalem became a battle ground between Christianity and Islam.

Jerusalem's rule then changed hands many times until the Mamluks, who ruled Jerusalem from Cairo, eventually defeated the Crusaders in 1247, and Jerusalem became a predominately Islamic city once more. In 1517, the Ottoman Empire conquered the Mamluks, and Süleyman the Magnificent (1520–1566) ruled over a period of prosperity in Jerusalem not seen since the days of Herod. Süleyman built the city walls that stand as the most distinctive feature of Jerusalem to this day. The Ottoman Turks retained control of Palestine (including Jerusalem) until the early twentieth century, but by then Jerusalem was a considerably weakened city.

Modern History

By the mid-nineteenth century, Jerusalem was again a city predominantly populated by Jews. It had also begun to expand beyond the walls of the old city into what are today districts of West Jerusalem. It remained under the control of a weakened Turkey, and European powers began to vie for control of the holy land. In 1917, British forces took control, declaring it the capital of the British Mandate of Palestine.

The British governed until 1947—but with increasing difficulty because of violent clashes between Jews and Arabs over the status of Palestine and Jerusalem. The UN intervened to try to calm the situation and proposed a plan in which Palestine would be divided into a Jewish and a Palestinian state. Jerusalem would remain an independent territory under the UN. The Palestinians rejected the plan, and when Jews declared an independent state of Israel following the withdrawal of the British in 1948, a war (the Arab-Israeli War) broke out between Israel and the Arab states of Jordan, Syria, and Egypt. At war's end, Jerusalem was split—Israel controlled West Jerusalem, and the country of Jordan controlled the old city and East Jerusalem.

Jerusalem remained divided until 1967, when the Six-Day War saw Israel regain all of Jerusalem and the territories that today make up the West Bank and the Gaza Strip. Israel has since expanded Jewish interests into East Jerusalem and beyond to consolidate its claim to Jerusalem as the undivided Israeli capital. The Palestinians refuse to recognize Israeli sovereignty over Jerusalem and proclaim that the city will one day be the capital of a Palestinian state.

▲ Israeli soldiers are seen here outside the UN offices in Jerusalem in June 1967. Israel gained control of Jordanian teritory, including East Jerusalem and the present-day West Bank, following the Six-Day War.

Renewed violence between Palestinians and Israelis since 2000 has dashed hopes of peace that were briefly raised in the 1990s, but a change in the Palestinian leadership, in January 2005, has revived talks between Israel and the Palestinian Authority. In February, the Israeli government began to hand back control of Israeli West Bank settlements to the Palestinians in a show of renewed cooperation. As long as there is no upsurge in violence, peace talks to discuss wide ranging issues, including the future of Jerusalem, are due to take place between the two sides during 2005.

People of Jerusalem

Jerusalem is Israel's most populous city, and its residents accounted for more than 10 percent of the Israeli population in 2002. When Israel was founded in 1948, Jerusalem had only 84,000 residents. As Jews arrived in Israel from around the world, Jerusalem quickly expanded, almost doubling its population to 167,400 by 1961. The incorporation of East Jerusalem in 1967 increased the population to 266,300 and significantly altered the structure of the population. Prior to 1967, the Arab population in Jerusalem was just 2,400 (1.5 percent), but the incorporation of East Jerusalem increased it to more than 68,000, or 25 percent of the city total.

"We see a trend . . . whereby the Arab population of Jerusalem continues to grow, and the Jewish population of the city continues to drop."

—Maya Choshen, *Statistical Yearbook of Jerusalem* 2003.

◄ *The narrow streets of Jerusalem's old city were once home to the entire population of the city. The first homes built beyond the city came in the mid-nineteenth century.*

Migration

During World War II (and immediately afterward), many European Jews sought refuge in what was then British Palestine in order to escape persecution under the German Nazis, who had a policy of exterminating Jews. From the late 1800s on, many Jews were drawn to Jerusalem (and all of Palestine) by the Jewish nationalist movement known as Zionism. These war refugees and survivors began the modern wave of immigration to Jerusalem, a wave that increased in pace following the creation of Israel in 1948 and the Israeli government's Law of Return, which stated that all Jews had a right to settle in Israel.

In this mass immigration, Jews came from across the world, but mainly from Arab states (Iraq, Morocco, Egypt, Tunisia, Libya, Syria, and Yemen, for example). This movement of Jews to their homeland is known as aliyah, meaning "going up," or ascending to Jerusalem. The most recent aliyah involved about eight hundred thousand olim ("ascenders") arriving between 1990 and 1999 from the countries of the former Soviet Union. These olim settled throughout Israel, but over the years they have added substantially to both the population and character of Jerusalem. Cultural influences, such as food and dress, now come from countries as widespread as Ethiopia, Russia, and Paraguay.

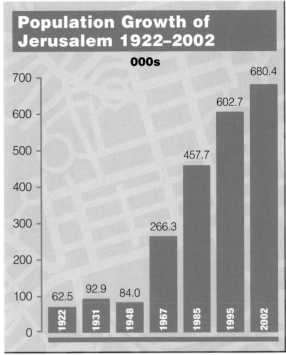

Source: Statistical Yearbook for Jerusalem 2003

Rapid Growth

Jerusalem's population has more than doubled since 1967, but the population growth of each culture has not been uniform. Between 1967 and 2002, the Jewish population did not increase as much as the Arab population did. The main reason is there have been more children born there to Arabs than to Jews. The faster increase in Jerusalem's Arab population means the proportion of Arabs in Jerusalem has increased substantially, from 25.6 percent in 1967 to 32.6 percent in 2002. If current trends continue, Arabs are expected to make up 38 percent of the city's population by 2020.

Jewish Settlement

With a growing Arab population, the Israeli government has actively encouraged the settlement of Jews in Jerusalem as a way to

▲ To celebrate the religious harvest festival of Sukkoth, the Jewish men in this procession are carrying bundles of palm, myrtle, and willow, together with a lemon-like fruit, as directed by the Torah (the Five Books of Moses). The procession is carrying the scrolls of the Torah to the Western Wall while singing in Hebrew.

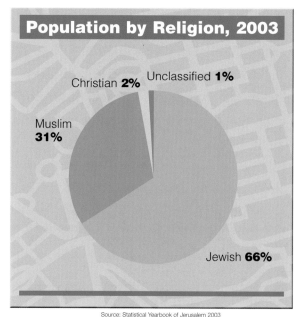

Population by Religion, 2003

Christian **2%**   Unclassified **1%**

Muslim **31%**

Jewish **66%**

Source: Statistical Yearbook of Jerusalem 2003

maintain a Jewish majority and safeguard a Jewish claim to the city. New Jewish settlements have been built around the fringes of the city, especially in land that, prior to 1967, was under Arab control. By the end of 2002, between 175,000 and 200,000 "settler Jews" lived in East

Jerusalem, and Jewish settlements continue to be built despite complaints from the Palestinians.

Religion

Jerusalem is a city built on—and divided by—religion. Religion enters into all aspects of city life, from what people eat to when they shop and when the city buses run. Jews make up the largest religious group in Jerusalem, accounting for 447,900 residents (66 percent) in early 2003. Of these, an estimated 135,000 are Haredi, an Orthodox Jewish group who live a very strict life according to the word of the Talmud, the Jewish book of civil and religious obedience. This obedience includes wearing appropriate clothing, following a kosher diet (food prepared according to the laws of Judaism), and not working on the Sabbath (even turning on a light switch is considered work).

▼ *The area around Damascus Gate, seen here, is the stronghold of the Muslim quarter of the old city and the gateway to East Jerusalem.*

Islam is Jerusalem's second-largest religion, with about 31 percent of the city's population being Muslims (most of them living in East Jerusalem). The Muslim population ranges from extremists opposed to the existence of Israel to ordinary residents and moderates who wish to build a lasting peace with their Jewish neighbors.

Jerusalem's Christian population is relatively small at only about 14,400 residents (just 2 percent of the total), and most of them are Arab Christians (about 12,000). The remainder of the population is unclassified in terms of religion, most of them being either nonreligious or a member

▼ *These bakers are making* matzo, *a flat, unleavened bread eaten especially during Pesach (see page 23).*

▶ *The diners pictured here are enjoying lunch at one of Jerusalem's many cafés. This café is located inside the Jaffa Gate of the old city.*

of one of hundreds of minority sects, some of which may only have a few members.

Food

Jerusalem's restaurants reflect the cuisines of the city's international settlers. Armenian, Hungarian, Mexican, Chinese, Indian, Italian, French, Ethiopian, Thai, Korean, and North African foods are among the different fares available. Local foods increasingly blend influences from across the Middle East and include dishes such as falafel (ground chickpeas mixed with herbs and spices, rolled into balls, and deep-fried); hummus

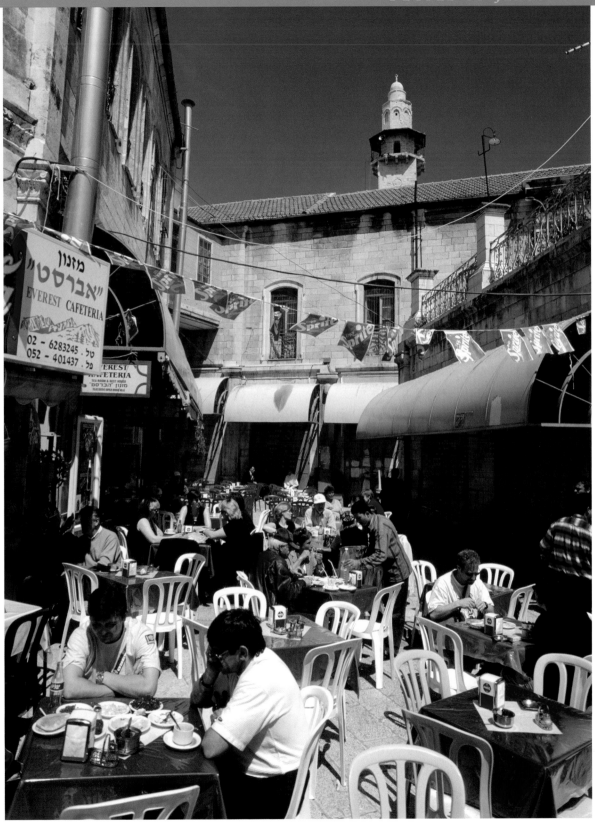

▲ *Street food is one of the main kinds of fare offered in Jerusalem. This vendor is in the Muslim quarter near the Damascus Gate.*

Food Rules

Both Islam and Judaism have dietary rules that influence the kinds of foods available in Jerusalem. Pork, for example, is banned under both Islamic and kosher rules, so it cannot be found in the markets of Jerusalem. The kosher diet (kashrut) also bans non-scaly fish (shellfish, squid, and so on) and states that all meat must be slaughtered in a particular way (shehita) and then washed and salted to drain it of all blood. Under kosher rules, meat must never be prepared with or eaten with dairy products, and separate crockery, cutlery, and utensils should be used for meat and dairy dishes. For this reason, a kosher restaurant serves either dairy or meat dishes but never both. Islam takes its dietary rules from the Koran, and it too prescribes that meat, known as halal meat, must be properly slaughtered and drained of blood. The laws of Islam also ban the drinking of alcohol.

(thick paste made from chickpeas); tahini (ground sesame seeds, garlic, lemon juice, and olive oil); *fuul* (fava bean stew); *shwarma* (warm meat sandwiches); and *shashlik* (grilled meat kebabs). *Mezze* (a mixed salad served with hummus, tahini, and pita bread) is especially popular in Jerusalem and takes advantage of the plentiful supply of fresh vegetables. Despite living in a largely desert state, Israel's farmers have mastered the use of irrigation technology to produce vast quantities of fresh produce that is consumed locally and exported.

Among Jerusalem's older residents of eastern and western European Jewish descent, traditional dishes are still the order of the day. Many restaurants still serve such "deli" fare as bagels with cream cheese and lox (a smoked salmon) and corned beef and hot pastrami sandwiches.

Celebrations

With so many different cultures and religions represented in Jerusalem, it seems that celebrations take place consistently throughout the year. The main Jewish celebrations include the observances of Rosh Hashanah (the Jewish New Year) and Yom Kippur (Day of Atonement), Hanukkah (Festival of Lights), Purim (*see page 41*), and Pesach (Passover, when the Angel of Death is believed to have passed over Jewish homes and when Moses led the Jews out of Egypt and slavery). For Muslims, Eid al-Adha (end of the Hajj, the pilgrimage to Mecca), the month of Ramadan, Eid al-Fitr (the day after Ramadan), and the prophet Mohammed's birthday are the main celebrations. Jerusalem's Christians celebrate Easter and Christmas. In addition to these, the people of Jerusalem observe the weekly holy days of Friday for Muslims, Saturday for Jews (from sunset Friday to sunset Saturday), and Sunday for Christians.

▼ *At Easter, pilgrims, such as these Nigerian Christians, follow the route along which Jesus is said to have carried his cross to the place where he was crucified. The Church of the Holy Sepulcher marks the site where many people believe Jesus was crucified, buried, and resurrected.*

CHAPTER 3

Living in Jerusalem

Although Jerusalemites mix for business, transportation, and shopping, the different communities around the city live separately from each other for much of the time. Housing is perhaps the most obvious division between Jerusalem's many people, but there are also splits in terms of health care and education, and the general standard of living also varies. The reality is a complex pattern of life that continues to change with the city's population and with the increasing number of new Jewish settlements in East Jerusalem that have been encouraged by the government.

Focus of Life

Until the mid-nineteenth century, the entire population of Jerusalem resided within the 1 square mile (2.6 sq km) formed by the walls of the old city. The land beyond the city walls was feared because of bandits and wolves. Population growth eventually led to overcrowding, however, and people were forced to leave the old city and begin settling in the hills and valleys beyond the city's walls. Mishkenot Sha'ananim was the first neighborhood to be built outside the

◀ *Silwan is one of the main Palestinian housing areas of Jerusalem. The housing here is dense and crowded in comparison to most Jewish neighborhoods.*

▲ *Orthodox Jews wear traditional dress in the strictly Orthodox Mea She'arim district of the city.*

old city in 1860, but by 1910, sixteen more neighborhoods had been built. Together, they had a population more than twice that of the old city. This "new" Jerusalem (beyond the city walls) has continued to expand ever since, and today it contains the main residential and commercial areas of the city. The old city continues to provide the symbolic focus for most city residents, however, and remains at the center of the competing claims to Jerusalem.

The division of the old city into four quarters or neighborhoods (Armenian, Christian, Jewish, and Muslim) is representative of the broader divisions that

"Suddenly, crowds of ordinary office workers are replaced by legions of men in black—black suits, black hats, [and] usually black ear locks [payos or forelocks]. Suddenly, they dominate the streets, and we bus riders move like time travelers from a bustling, modern city into an eighteenth-century Jewish village in Poland and then quickly back to modernity."

—Robert Fulford, describing a trip through the Mea She'arim neighborhood in *Globe and Mail*, June 4, 1997.

◀ *In addition to supermarkets common to any large city, Jerusalem also has a variety of smaller markets that are an important part of daily life for the people living there as well as an attraction for visitors. This indoor market thrives in the Muslim quarter of the old city. These underground markets have been in existence almost as long as the city itself.*

affect the city and the country. On the whole, however, the old city is a peaceful part of Jerusalem, popular with tourists and with pilgrims who come to visit its many religious sites. Motor vehicles are banished from much of the old city and would not, in any case, fit down some of the narrow alleyways. Instead, the alleyways bustle with pedestrians visiting cafés, souvenir shops, and markets.

Neighborhoods

As Jerusalem developed beyond the city walls, people drew together according to social groups and settled in what became distinct neighborhoods. This pattern continued throughout the nineteenth and much of the twentieth century and led to

"True, [Jerusalem] was physically reunited in 1967 when the walls were torn down during the Six-Day War. But socially the city remains divided today as if the walls were still there."

—Simon Griver, *Insight Guide to Jerusalem*, 1998.

neighborhoods such as the German Colony, the Russian Compound, and the Palestinian town of Silwan. Since the reunification of Jerusalem in 1967, many of the neighborhoods have become less defined, but some still preserve a unique character.

Among the most unique of these neighborhoods is Mea She'arim, to the northwest of the old city, which was established in 1873 by Haredi concerned about the modern world destroying the basis of their faith. Mea She'arim remains a strictly Orthodox community today and isolates itself from the modern world by banning radios, televisions, and even newspapers. Signs warn visitors to dress conservatively (showing as little skin as possible), and those who fail to observe the dress code risk verbal abuse and some have even had stones thrown at them.

Another peculiarity of Mea She'arim is that many of its residents speak Yiddish, a language once widely spoken by Jews in the villages, neighborhoods, and ghettos of eastern Europe. Yiddish is written in Hebrew characters but contains elements of German, Slavic, and Hebrew dialects. Most Jews in Israel today are more familiar with Hebrew, English, and other languages (including Arabic) than with Yiddish, which they may associate with the culture of oppression and death that followed many Jews fleeing to Palestine from Nazi Germany in the 1930s and 1940s. Residents of Mea She'arim continue to speak Yiddish, however, in the belief that Hebrew, the language spoken by

"We break up Arab continuity and their claim to East Jerusalem by putting in isolated islands of Jewish presence in areas of Arab population."

—Uri Bank, a leader of the pro-settlement Moledet Party, 2003.

the majority of Jews in Israel, should be reserved solely for prayer and not used as an everyday language.

Housing

Although Jerusalem has a small population by world standards, it is a relatively crowded city, and housing is in short supply. Therefore, housing density (number of people per household) is higher in Jerusalem than elsewhere in Israel. In 2003, Jerusalem had an average housing density of 3.4 people compared to 2.3 people in the city of Tel Aviv and 3.1 people in Israel as a whole. The variations are even more marked when the difference between Jews and non-Jews (mainly Palestinian Arabs) is considered. For Jews, there were an average of 3.3 people per household in 2001. Non-Jewish households, however, had an average of 5.8 people per household, and more than one-third of these households (36.3 percent) had more than 7 people living in them.

Housing is a highly controversial issue in Jerusalem. Since gaining control of East Jerusalem, the Israeli government has actively promoted the construction of new Jewish settlements there but has, at the same

▼ *As Jerusalem's population continues to expand, new Jewish settlements are being constructed beyond the city boundaries in the West Bank. Palestinians are concerned that such construction will lead to an expansion of the area that Israel claims as Jerusalem.*

Preserving Jerusalem

One of the most noticeable things about Jerusalem is its remarkably uniform appearance. This uniformity is the result of strict planning and architectural guidelines that were introduced about 1918, during the period of British control. The guidelines stated that all buildings should be faced with Jerusalem stone so as to preserve the architectural heritage of the city. During the period 1948 to 1965, rapid population growth made the creation of new housing more important than the appearance of the buildings, and the guidelines were largely ignored. In 1965, however, Mayor Teddy Kollek, who presided over Jerusalem between 1965 and 1993, reinstated the guidelines, and it is he who is largely responsible for the visual harmony of the city today.

time, placed quotas (limits) or complex bureaucracy in the way of Palestinian housing developments. Many Palestinians refuse to apply for permits to build new houses because they believe it would indicate acceptance of Israel's sovereignty over East Jerusalem. As a result, their houses are built illegally and run the risk of being bulldozed by the Israeli authorities.

Education

Jerusalem is a major education center and home to Israel's most prestigious university, the Hebrew University of Jerusalem. Originally opened in 1925, the university was located at Mount Scopus in East Jerusalem but forced to relocate in 1948, when the war left East Jerusalem under Jordanian control. New campuses were built in West Jerusalem, but when the city was reunited in 1967, the Mount Scopus campus was rebuilt and is again the main site of the university today. In 2003, the university had 22,600 students enrolled (almost 20 percent of all of Israel's students) and a staff of about 2,700.

Al-Quds, an Arab university, has several campuses to the east and north of the old city and provides a center of learning for the Palestinian community. The idea of a Palestinian university in Jerusalem had been discussed since the 1930s, but political tensions and problems about where to locate the university meant it did not actually come into existence until 1995, when several colleges completed a merger, or joining together, a process that began in 1984. By 2004, Al-Quds University had about 5,250 students and was continuing to develop rapidly. Its plans for growth could be jeopardized, however, by Israeli plans to further expand the municipal boundaries of Jerusalem. If this were to happen, then part of the university grounds may be confiscated to make way for a new road.

Several school systems operate in Jerusalem, each offering a slightly different form of education. The biggest system is run by the Jerusalem Education Authority and had about 102,000 students in 2002–2003. Most of these (about 61.5 percent) were in

▲ *This bilingual school educates both Jewish and Arab children and encourages them to grow up together in peace.*

public Hebrew education with the remainder being in public Arab education. In addition to the public education system, Jerusalem has many private schools taught in either Hebrew or Arabic. In 2002–2003, there were 20,363 pupils in private Arab education and 78,545 pupils in Orthodox Hebrew schools. The number of students in Arab education has increased dramatically in recent years, as Palestinians have accounted for an increasing proportion of Jerusalem's population. Between 1998 and 2003, the number of pupils in the Arab education system (municipal and private) grew by 43 percent. No matter which system students follow, most will receive one to two years of preschool (kindergarten), six years of elementary school (grades 1–6), and six years of high school (grades 7–12).

Health Care

Jerusalem has many hospitals, including some that provide specific services for the Haredi and the Palestinian communities. The Hadassah Medical Center is the city's most prestigious hospital and has a reputation as one of the most advanced hospitals in the world. With more than one thousand beds and thirty-eight hundred staff, the hospital treated more than one million people in 2002. The municipal public health department provides a network of about thirty-five community clinics that offer treatment focused on the young, the elderly, and mothers and babies. In addition, doctors and nurses from the public health department visit the city's schools to conduct health and dental checks and immunization services.

▼ *The facilities at the Haddasah Medical Center are among the best in the world, and people travel from throughout Israel and beyond for treatment there.*

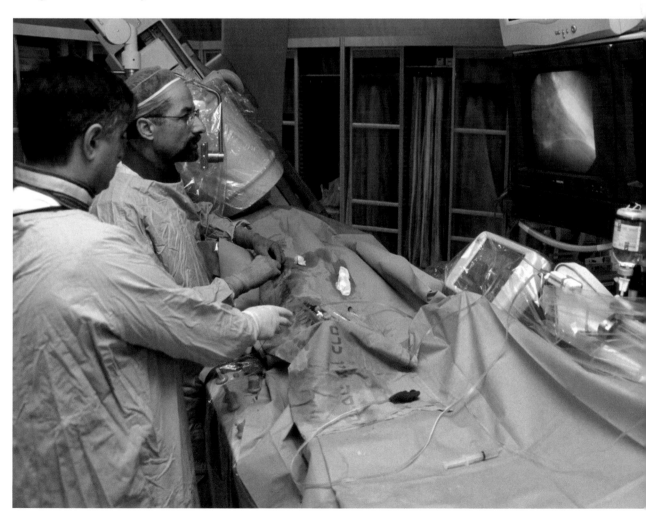

Poverty

In 2002, Jerusalem had a higher proportion of households (32.5 percent) living in poverty than the rest of Israel (18.1 percent). The low socioeconomic status of Jerusalem's Arab and Haredi communities is the main reason for this high level, because those communities tend to have larger families, less participation in the workforce, and lower average incomes. The Jerusalem municipality has a social services department that offers benefits and services to help those living in poverty. In 2002–2003, it assisted almost 129,000 people, or 19 percent of the city population. A slightly higher proportion of Haredi

▼ *Jerusalem's old city is an almost vehicle-free area, but elsewhere traffic congestion can be a problem, as seen here along the Jaffa Road.*

households (24.9 percent) and Arab households (24.6 percent) received support from social services compared to other household groups in the city (23 percent).

Transportation

Jerusalem suffers regular traffic congestion, and the city authorities continue to search for ways to improve accessibility for the city's growing population. Linking new settlements to the city center and to each other is particularly important but often leads to controversy over the placement of new transportation routes. The volume of

> "Right now it may seem like a no-man's-land, but with the 13.8-kilometer [9-mile] line from Pisgat Ze'ev to Mount Herzl using Jaffa Road as its main artery, you will see cafés, restaurants, commercial buildings, and new housing flourishing in the downtown area. We expect this part of Jerusalem to look like many European cities, where residents who normally can afford other means of transportation use the light railway because of its ease, thus creating a new urban environment."
>
> —Eitan Meir, chairman of Jerusalem's Mass Transit Project, 2002.

Jerusalem Mass Transit Project

In 2001, Jerusalem city authorities, together with international and Israeli companies, began the first stages of the Jerusalem Mass Transit Project. The centerpiece of the project is a new light-rail system that will run through the city in the hope of relieving traffic congestion. At the peak of rush hour in Jerusalem, buses can be reduced to traveling at speeds of just 3 miles per hour (5 k/ph). The light-rail system will begin operating one line in 2007 and is scheduled to have eight lines covering 34 miles (54 km) by 2020. Each light-rail car will carry up to five hundred passengers, and stations along the route will be met by feeder buses and have parking facilities that will allow people to park their cars and ride. Cycling will also be encouraged as part of Jerusalem's plan to revitalize transportation in the city.

motorized traffic on the city roads increased more than threefold between 1980 and 2001—from 42,517 registered vehicles to 141,007, with about 78 percent of all vehicles being private cars. The Israeli bus cooperative (called Egged) provides bus services with flat-fare rates for journeys within Jerusalem. Various Palestinian companies run bus services in East Jerusalem and to the West Bank settlements nearby. Taxis and shared taxis, known as *sheruts*, offer an alternative to the bus and provide access to more remote parts of the city.

CHAPTER 4

Jerusalem at Work

The majority of Jerusalem's residents work in the service industries, mostly within the government (national and local), education, health, social, and community services. In fact, almost 49 percent of the 217,300 people employed in Jerusalem in 2001–2002 worked for these public services, compared to just 27 percent in the same sectors in Tel Aviv and 33 percent nationally. By contrast, Jerusalem has a poorly developed industrial or manufacturing sector compared to other Israeli cities such as Tel Aviv and Haifa. The industries it does have include textiles, publishing, printing, electronics, and biotechnology. Small-scale manufacturing of jewelry, furniture, metalwork, and pottery can also be found in Jerusalem. In the bazaars of the old city, artisans make and sell a variety of tourist souvenirs.

Tourism

Tourism is a key service industry in Jerusalem, providing thousands of jobs for such people as hotel staff, tour guides, restaurant workers, taxi drivers, souvenir sellers, and so on. Up until 2000, about 75 percent of all tourists in Israel would spend time in Jerusalem, visiting its religious and

◀ *The Israeli Prime Minister, Ariel Sharon, speaks at the Knesset in 2001. The Knesset is the seat of the Israeli parliament that is located in Jerusalem.*

▶ *Violent conflict between the Palestinians and Israelis has caused a drop in the number of tourists visiting Jerusalem in recent years. Some souvenir stores, such as this one in West Jerusalem, offer discounts for "brave" tourists.*

Open for Business

The workday begins early in Jerusalem, with most offices opening about 8:00 A.M. A traditional lunch break followed by a rest period finds most banks and smaller stores and offices closed between 1:00 P.M. and 4:00 P.M. Larger stores and offices tend to remain open. The work day ends about 7:00 P.M., but some stores stay open later into the evening. The Jewish work week is Sunday through Thursday. Saturday is the Sabbath, and virtually all of West Jerusalem is closed. Banks, government offices, and many businesses are also closed on Friday (as they would be on a Sunday in the United States), but shops and restaurants tend to stay open until late Friday afternoon when Shabbat, the Jewish Sabbath, begins at sunset. Most restaurants, cafés, bars, and some stores will reopen for a few hours after sunset on Saturday (the end of Shabbat). In Palestinian East Jerusalem, businesses remain open most of the time, although some may close on Friday for the Muslim day of rest and worship and/or on Sunday for the Christian Sabbath. All faiths tend to close their businesses for their respective holy days and festivals, and Muslims observe shorter working hours during the holy month of Ramadan.

historic sites. Tourism benefited both Palestinians and Israelis, and so the city put into place conditions that helped keep Jerusalem a relatively safe and peaceful city. In 2000, however, as part of an uprising called the *intifada*, Palestinian terrorists targeted crowded buses and public places in Jerusalem. As a result of this violence, tourism in Jerusalem collapsed. In 2002, the number of foreign tourists staying in hotels in Jerusalem fell to just 189,100 compared to 895,500 in 2000—a decline of almost 80 percent. By mid-2003, increased security measures made Jerusalem safer, and tourism was showing signs of recovery. Any improvement is likely to be slow, however, because the threat of further violence remains.

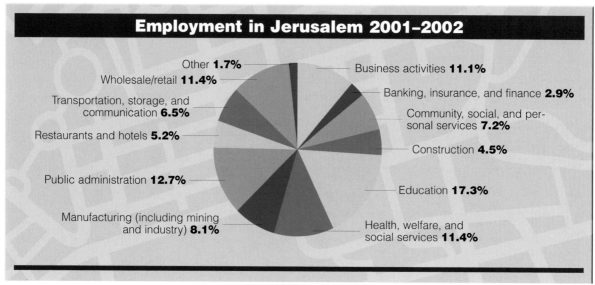

Employment in Jerusalem 2001–2002

Other **1.7%**
Wholesale/retail **11.4%**
Transportation, storage, and communication **6.5%**
Restaurants and hotels **5.2%**
Public administration **12.7%**
Manufacturing (including mining and industry) **8.1%**

Business activities **11.1%**
Banking, insurance, and finance **2.9%**
Community, social, and personal services **7.2%**
Construction **4.5%**
Education **17.3%**
Health, welfare, and social services **11.4%**

Source: Statistical Yearbook of Jerusalem 2003

Seat of Government

Jerusalem is the seat of the Israeli government and home to many of the country's national institutes. The Israeli parliament building, the Knesset, lies to the west of the old city in a green area called Givat Ram. The Supreme Court, the Bank of Israel, the prime minister's offices, museums, and a campus of the Hebrew University are also located here. The parliament consists of 120 members who are elected every four years by proportional representation. In a system of proportional representation, the number of seats a political party gets in parliament is based on the percentage of votes it receives in the overall election. In Israel, for example, parties representing the interests of various minority groups, such as ultra-Orthodox Jews or Israeli Arabs, may win seats in parliament despite their relatively small numbers in the nation as a whole. The prime minister heads the government and is elected directly by the people. All Israeli citizens over eighteen years of age are entitled to vote.

The mayor and a local council of thirty members govern the municipality of Jerusalem. Both the mayor and the council are elected every four years. Although Palestinians residing in East Jerusalem are entitled to vote and run in local council elections, most boycott the elections because they refuse to recognize Israeli control of East Jerusalem.

"We have the right to go to the Orient House. We have the right to go anywhere we want in Palestine, including Jerusalem."

—Hanan Ashrawi, senior Palestinian talking after the Israeli occupation and closure of New Orient House, August 2001

New Orient House

Located in the Sheikh Jarrah quarter to the north of the old city, New Orient House is the headquarters for the Palestine Liberation Organization (PLO) in East Jerusalem. It serves as a focal point for Palestinian demands for an independent state with Jerusalem as its capital. Its location within Israeli-controlled Jerusalem has been the cause of much tension between the Israeli government and the Palestinians. The Israelis closed New Orient House between 1988 and 1992, claiming its activities were a threat to Israeli security. In 1999, the Palestinian Authority met with a delegation of the European Union in New Orient House and caused outrage among many Israelis who saw this as a direct threat to their control of Jerusalem. In August 2001, at the height of the latest intifada, New Orient House was raided by the Israelis, its contents confiscated, and its doors closed once again. This picture (below) shows Israeli police outside New Orient House arresting a protester at one of the angry demonstrations that followed this most recent closure. It remains closed today, despite Palestinian and international calls for it to be reopened as a base from which the Palestinians can enter into peace negotiations with Israel.

CHAPTER 5

Jerusalem at Play

With its diverse population, Jerusalem is a city bursting with cultural interest, from its religious sites to its architecture to its numerous museums that portray different aspects of the city's long and complex history. Theater, dance, movies, concerts, and art are among the other cultural attractions to be found in Jerusalem. The city also has public parks, nature areas, and plenty of cafés and restaurants.

Museums

Jerusalem's museums display hundreds of thousands of exhibits. One of the most famous museums is the Israel Museum, which celebrates the cultural and historical heritage of Israel. The museum opened in 1965 and receives about 950,000 visitors every year. It contains about 500,000 items in several buildings, including the *Dead Sea Scrolls* in the distinctive Shrine of the Book building. The *Dead Sea Scrolls*, found in 1947 by a shepherd boy near Qumran, are the oldest Biblical relics ever found. No one is quite sure of their significance, and debate continues over their precise meaning.

Other important museums in Jerusalem include the Islamic Museum in the old city, which is the oldest museum in the city and

◄ *A youth enjoys a game of soccer. Despite the popularity of this and other sports in Jerusalem, there are relatively few sports facilities in the city.*

▲ *The dome-shaped Shrine of the Book building in West Jerusalem houses the Dead Sea Scrolls. It is designed to resemble the lids of the jars that contained the Scrolls when a young boy found them in 1947.*

includes collections of coins, ceramics, military items, and beautifully calligraphied copies of the Koran. Also in the old city is the Tower of David Museum that tells the dramatic history of Jerusalem. Yad Vashem, or the Holocaust Museum, in the west of the city, provides a memorial for the more than six million Jews who were exterminated by the German Nazis during World War II.

Art and Music

Many of Jerusalem's finest works of art are housed within its various museums or in prominent buildings such as the Knesset and Hadassah Medical Center. Performance arts and music, however, have their own venues. The Jerusalem Center for Performing Arts, to the west of the old city, is a major arts complex with two theaters and an auditorium that is home to the Jerusalem Symphony Orchestra. It hosts drama, dance, opera, and regular classical music concerts. The Palestinian National Theater in East Jerusalem provides a stage for Palestinian

Marc Chagall (1887–1985)

One of the most celebrated Jewish artists is Marc Chagall. Chagall was born in Russia and spent time living in France and the United States. He never lived in Israel, but he gave the state, and Jerusalem in particular, many of his finest works. These include the tapestries that hang in the Knesset building and his painting "The Rabbi" in the Israel Museum. His most celebrated work in Jerusalem, however, is the Chagall Windows. These twelve stained-glass windows are installed in the synagogue of the Hadassah Medical Center in Ein Kerem. Each is a different color and represents one of the twelve tribes of Israel, the twelve original clans of ancient Hebrews descended from the twelve sons of Jacob.

cultural and artistic expression and also runs various cultural education programs. One of its annual highlights is an international puppet festival—a favorite with children.

Beneath the walls of the old city, the Sultan's Pool Amphitheater provides a dramatic stage for outdoor music concerts during the summer and has hosted stars such as Bob Dylan and Placido Domingo. Numerous movie theaters in Jerusalem show a mix of Hollywood and European movies. The Cinemathèque, southwest of the old city walls, is a small theater and coffee house that shows older and more unusual movies. Cinemathèque also hosts the annual Jerusalem movie festival in June and July, showing movies from around the world.

Sports

Jerusalem's Orthodox Haredi community disapproves of sports. This was most clearly seen in a near twenty-year battle to construct a soccer stadium in Jerusalem for the local team, Betar Jerusalem. Mayor Teddy Kollek eventually succeeded in overcoming their opposition, and the Teddy Kollek Soccer Stadium was opened in 1992. Soccer matches are played weekly and accompanied by much singing, chanting, and horn blowing from the crowd. Basketball is an equally lively spectator sport. The local team, Hapoel Jerusalem, normally plays on Sundays in the Malkha district of West Jerusalem.

For the public, hotels offer sports facilities, as do the local gyms. An Olympic-size swimming pool is open to the public, and tennis and cycling clubs are available.

Public Parks

Sacher Park is the largest of Jerusalem's approximately eight hundred public parks, gardens, and open spaces. Other well-known areas include Independence Park in downtown West Jerusalem, the Wohl Rose Garden next to the Knesset, and the Botanical Gardens on the Givat Ram campus of the Hebrew University. The Jerusalem forest stretches to the west of the city and is said to contain six million trees to mark the victims who perished in the Holocaust. Jerusalem is also developing urban nature areas within its municipal boundary such as Pri-Har Valley (valley of the deer) in which a herd of about twenty-five wild deer can be observed.

Festivals

Jerusalemites are able to relax and enjoy themselves during festivals and celebrations. For Muslims of East Jerusalem, the Islamic feast of Eid al-Fitr is one of the most anticipated celebrations, marking the end of the holy month of Ramadan. Families gather for communal prayers (*Salat*) and to share food and gifts. It is also traditional to buy new clothes for the occasion and to visit the graves of relatives.

In mainly Jewish West Jerusalem, one of the most enjoyable of all the festivals is Purim. This celebrates a Biblical story from the fifth century B.C., in which Esther (the queen of Persia and a Jew) saved her fellow Jews from execution by Haman, a chief minister of the Persian king. It is celebrated by reading the Megillah (scroll). Children are encouraged to interrupt the reading with noisemakers each time Haman's name is mentioned—fifty-four times in all. Later, a family meal including sweet pastries called *hamantaschen* ("Haman's ears") is shared. Families, and especially children, dress up in costumes of the story's characters, and the streets take on a carnival atmosphere as people celebrate the Purim story.

▼ *These children are dressed up to watch a reenactment of the story of Esther saving Persian Jews from Haman. The enactment is part of one of Judaism's brightest celebrations, the Purim festival.*

CHAPTER 6

Looking Forward

Jerusalem seems set to continue its growth and expansion over the coming decades, but the precise nature of this growth remains to be seen. The city continues to be at the heart of the ongoing tensions and conflicts between Israel and the Palestinians. Moves toward peace in the 1990s have been replaced with an escalation of violence in the new millennium, and Jerusalem has paid a high price with lives lost and its tourist industry badly damaged. Whether Jerusalem can become a city of peace in the twenty-first century remains very much unknown and a tremendous challenge for its people.

Violence and Security

The most recent intifada by Palestinians has turned Jerusalem into a city on alert. From the start of 2000 up until the end of September 2003, Jerusalem and the immediate area experienced 129 terrorist attacks, killing 261 people and injuring 1,495. This count is more deaths and injuries than in the entire thirty-two years, between 1967 and 1999, following Israel's capture of East Jerusalem. In response to these attacks, Jerusalem has been among the first parts of the country to be fenced in by a controversial

◄ *Israel's controversial security fence, seen here in the background, cuts off the Palestinian village of Abu Dis in the West Bank from East Jerusalem. Palestinians frequently protest against the construction of the barrier that divides the communities.*

> *"I live in downtown Jerusalem. There was that terrorist attack a couple of years ago when someone started firing a rifle all over the place. That's got to affect you. I don't identify myself as an Israeli or as a Jew, just a Jerusalemite. I was born here and that's all I know. I prefer a self-made identity, not a national or religious identity."*

—Roy Assiag (a.k.a. Rocky B), twenty-four-year-old Jerusalemite rapper, 2004.

▲ *Israeli prime minister Ariel Sharon (left) shakes hands with Palestinian president Mahmoud Abbas at peace talks in Egypt in February 2005. The future status of Jerusalem remains a major obstacle in talks between the two sides.*

Israeli security fence. The fence separates Jerusalem from other parts of the country and in particular divides Palestinian communities. It also limits the movement of Palestinians into and out of East Jerusalem. Palestinians claim it is a breach of their rights, but the Israeli government argues the fence is needed to prevent further terrorist attacks.

The Settlement Question

Israel is pursuing its policy of building new Jewish settler homes in both West and, more controversially, East Jerusalem. To the Israeli government, these new settlements confirm Israel's claim to all of Jerusalem as their capital. Palestinians, however, resent the construction, especially when they are subjected to strict building limits. Many Palestinians remain insistent that East Jerusalem will one day be the capital of an independent Palestinian state.

New Hope

In January 2005, Mahmoud Abbas replaced the deceased Yasser Arafat as the leader of the Palestinian Authority. The change of leadership among the Palestinians has generated hope for renewed peace talks with Israel, but the Israeli prime minister, Ariel Sharon, has made it clear that he will not negotiate until Palestinian terrorist attacks on Jerusalem and other Israeli targets stop. The more extreme Palestinian groups responsible for such attacks appear to be backing Abbas, but unless there is real and rapid progress toward a Palestinian state, many Middle East experts fear the violence will return. Jerusalem has, in the past, been a major stumbling block in peace talks, with neither side willing to give up their claim to the city. If those differences could be overcome, then Jerusalem could one day stand as a pattern of peace and coexistence to be followed throughout the world.

Time Line

c. 3000–2500 B.C. Evidence of first human settlements around the area of Gihon Spring.

c. 2000–1400 B.C. Ancient Egyptian texts refer to Jerusalem as a city-state.

1000 B.C. David unites the twelve tribes of Judah and Israel, making Jerusalem his capital.

953 B.C. David's son Solomon completes the First Temple of Jerusalem on Mount Moriah.

586 B.C. King Nebuchadnezzer of Babylonia destroys the First Temple and exiles the Jews from Jerusalem.

538 B.C. Under Persian control, the Jews return to Jerusalem and rebuild their temple.

333 B.C. The armies of Alexander the Great arrive in Jerusalem, and the city passes peacefully into the control of the Greek empire under the Ptolemies of Egypt.

198 B.C. The Greek Seleucids gain control of Jerusalem and transform it into a Greek city.

167–164 B.C. The Jews revolt, after which their Hasmonean dynasty controls the city.

63 B.C. The Roman Empire invades and conquers Jerusalem.

4 B.C. Jerusalem passes into the hands of Roman procurators.

A.D. 33 Jesus is crucified in Jerusalem.

66–70 A Jewish uprising against Roman rule is finally quashed when the Romans storm Jerusalem and destroy the city.

135 Emperor Hadrian levels Jerusalem and builds a new city, Aelia Capitolina.

638 Jerusalem is invaded by Muslim armies under Caliph Omar, ending Roman rule of the city.

1099 A series of Christian Crusades begin that are fought to regain Christian access to Jerusalem from its Muslim rulers.

1247 The Mamluks of Egypt defeat the Crusaders and take control of Jerusalem.

1517 Jerusalem becomes a city of the Turkish Ottoman Empire. Süleyman the Magnificent builds the existing city walls.

1917 The British take control of Jerusalem and make it capital of the British Mandate of Palestine.

1947–48 The United Nations tries to negotiate a deal between Jews and Arabs over the sharing of Palestine. The Palestinian Arabs reject the deal.

1948 The state of Israel is declared following British withdrawal from Palestine. This triggers the Arab-Israeli War in which Israel extends its territory in the region.

1967 Israel responds to threats on its borders by launching the Six-Day War against Egypt, Jordan, and Syria and gains control of additional territory that today makes up Gaza, the West Bank, and East Jerusalem.

2000 A renewed *intifada* by Palestinian factions causes violence across Israel.

2004 Palestinian leader Yasser Arafat dies and is replaced by Mahmoud Abbas in 2005. Hopes for peace talks are renewed.

Glossary

aliyah the journey and arrival of new immigrants in the Jewish state of Israel. It means "stepping up" to the Temple Mount in Jerusalem.

boycott refusal to buy from or deal in a commercial way with a country or organization as a form of protest.

bureaucracy a system of organizational departments, their officials, and the way they do business.

Caliph the title given to a Muslim ruler who is said to have authority on behalf of Mohammed.

calligraphied written in a practiced and stylized handwriting that is quite beautiful.

city-state an independent state made up of a city and the surrounding area.

congestion overcrowded conditions.

Crusades military expeditions authorized by the pope (the head of the Roman Catholic church) during the eleventh, twelfth, and thirteenth centuries to take over from the Muslims the land where Jesus lived and died.

ear locks (also called *payos* or forelocks) long, usually curled, sideburns worn by some Orthodox Jews who believe the Torah commands them not to cut or shave them.

Haredi Orthodox Jews who strictly follow the teachings of the Talmud.

Hebrew the official language of Israel, also spoken by Jewish communities beyond Israel, particularly for religious events.

Holocaust huge destruction and loss of life; capitalized, the term is often used to describe the mass killings of Jews by the German Nazis during World War II.

ideological based upon or relating to a particular set of ideas, values, opinions, or beliefs that influences the way an individual or group thinks and acts.

immigrants people who move into a new country and settle there.

intifada Arabic word used to describe the Palestinian uprising against the continued Israeli occupation of lands the Palestinian people believe to be rightfully theirs.

Islam a major world religion that started in the seventh century in Arabia. Islam is practiced by Muslims, who believe in submission to God and in Mohammad as the chief and last prophet of God.

kosher (food) prepared for consumption or sold according to the dietary rules of Judaism; also used to describe an establishment selling such foods.

mosque a place of worship for Muslims.

municipal relating to a town or city and sometimes its surrounding area. Municipal is normally used to describe the local government system for that town or city.

Muslims individuals who follow the religion of Islam.

Ottoman relating to members of Turkish tribes in the late twelfth century under their leader Osman.

persecution injury or harassment due to a difference in religion, country of origin, skin color, or other factors.

pilgrimage a journey, usually made for a religious purpose, such as visiting a holy place.

procurators administrators with legal powers in the Roman Empire. Procurators were often appointed by Rome to govern the far reaches of the empire.

Ptolemies a dynasty of rulers from Macedonia who ruled Egypt and neighboring territories from 323–30 B.C.

Sabbath the seventh day of the week; a day of rest and worship, observed on Fridays by Muslims, Saturdays by Jews, and Sundays by most Christians.

Seljuk Turks nomadic tribes from central Asia who converted to Islam in the 900s; migrated west, conquering as they went.

Slavic describes people originally from the area of the Ukraine and Poland and who speak similar Slavic or Slavonic languages.

United Nations an organization of nations founded in 1945 to promote peace, security, and economic development.

Further Information

Books

Brooke, Steven. *Views of Jerusalem and the Holy Land*. Rizzoli, 1998.

Hellander, Paul and Andrew Humphreys. *Jerusalem*. Lonely Planet Publications, 1999.

Henty, G. A. *For the Temple*. Lost Classics Book Co.; Reprint edition 2001.

Jerusalem and the Holy Land. Eyewitness Travel Guides (series). Dorling Kindersley, 2000.

Waldman, Neil. *Golden City: Jerusalem's 3,000 Years*. Boyds Mills Press, 2000.

Web Sites

www.imj.org.il
Explore exhibits, programs, and resources from the Israel Museum in Jerusalem.

www.jerusalem.muni.il
Jerusalem's municipal government shares sites, events, and arts and culture of the capital city.

www.jiis.org.il
This Jerusalem Institute for Israeli Studies Web site links to statistics and the annual yearbook of Jerusalem.

www.md.huji.ac.il/special/chagall/chagall.html
View the famous Chagall windows of Jerusalem and read about how the artist created them. Click on each one to see it enlarged and read its inscription.

www.md.huji.ac.il/special/vjt
View the gates of Jerusalem, holy sites, and more.

Index